THE MASSACRE CONFIRMED OUR WORST SUSPICIONS

ESSENTIAL POETS SERIES 267

Canada Council for the Arts
Conseil des Arts du Canada

ONTARIO ARTS COUNCIL
CONSEIL DES ARTS DE L'ONTARIO

an Ontario government agency
un organisme du gouvernement de l'Ont

Canada

Guernica Editions Inc. acknowledges the support of the Canada Council for the Arts and the Ontario Arts Council. The Ontario Arts Council is an agency of the Government of Ontario.

We acknowledge the financial support of the Government of Canada.

THE MASSACRE CONFIRMED OUR WORST SUSPICIONS

W.B. MacDONALD

GUERNICA EDITIONS

TORONTO – BUFFALO – LANCASTER (U.K.)
2018

Michael Mirolla, editor
Interior design: Errol F. Richardson
Cover design: Justin Baker
Author photo: Anne Walsh
Guernica Editions Inc.
1569 Heritage Way, Oakville, (ON), Canada L6M 2Z7
2250 Military Road, Tonawanda, N.Y. 14150-6000 U.S.A.
www.guernicaeditions.com

Distributors:
University of Toronto Press Distribution,
5201 Dufferin Street, Toronto (ON), Canada M3H 5T8
Gazelle Book Services, White Cross Mills
High Town, Lancaster LA1 4XS U.K.

First edition.
Printed in Canada.

Legal Deposit – Third Quarter
Library of Congress Catalog Card Number: 2018953755
Library and Archives Canada Cataloguing in Publication
MacDonald, Bruce, 1956-, author
The massacre confirmed our worst suspicions / W.B. MacDonald.

(Essential poets series ; 267)
ISBN 978-1-77183-408-7 (softcover)

I. Title. II. Series: Essential poets series ; 267

PS8625.D6248M37 2018 C811'.6 C2018-904632-5

Dear Reader

This poetry of mine
is a large estate
I will never own.
It is a Rolls-Royce
I will never drive.
It is a Paris apartment
for a woman half my age.
It is a cellar of vintages
I will never drink.
You will agree,
this poetry of mine
is a rather
expensive hobby.

Contents

Royal City Rhapsody

O city of the loyal order of odd sons of the lodge of the
free Christian moose assembly pioneers of the 7th dan
empire black belt society of auto body pizza parlour
fellowship vagabonds! O spinster city! O rain drenched city!
O Lucky Lager city! O city by the Fraser River!
O New Westminster! O most royal city!

O city of awe spoiling churches of gothic ships'
captains' quarters of clapboard and gingerbread of
turrets and steeples and wrought iron widows' walks of
walls of laurel of forlorn monkey puzzle trees of the
astringent stink of sawn cedar and freight cars rutting
in the switching yards by the docks of the grottoes of
The Royal Towers Hotel of the King Edward Hotel of
the Dunsmuir Hotel of the Terminal City Hotel of
the College Hotel of pickled eggs in specimen jars and
waiters sullen as hospital orderlies slinging two-bits a
glass green foamless tap swill on sodden red terry
towel table prophylactics—O city of another round
and last call and off sales of silicate slippery shuffle-
board and bent cues and worn felt and narrow pockets
of table hopping waiters dumping ashtrays into two
quart tin cans of constables picking their way through
the boozy rabble—

O city of the BC Penitentiary of ersatz castle parapets and
guard towers of forty-foot walls and barbed wire—
O city of the mid-Victorian late medieval gothic
Enlightenment Henry the Eighth Austro-Hungarian
gingerbread mock Renaissance style of the returning
war hero baby boom bungalow of the Queen Anne

shoe box of the Tudor Chevrolet and the Craftsman
fixer upper—O city of gables and exposed beams of
cedar shingle and shake of stucco and false half
timbering—O city of the permanent upper story
vacancy and lower discount furniture and second hand
appliance dealer—O city of '50s false fronts and signage
and vinyl siding—O where is the stripping wind to restore
King Edward the Fifth and Mary Pickford to the throne?

O city of moss in every fissure crack and chink of
moss in every shade and every shadow of moss on
anything unmoving of moss in every cleft crack and
crevice in every niche fold fissure and interstice of
moss high and low—O city of the moss-bordered of
the moss-trimmed of the moss-edged of the moss-hemmed
and of moss on moss—O city of the long-striding
street-haunting half-wit waving enthusiastically at passing
cars—
O city of the incarcerated father of the alcoholic mother
of the pox-marked thug—O city of the amputee of
the divorcee of the ladies hospital auxiliary—O city
of roving bands of the mentally retarded of ears too
low and heads too big and spastic limbs and gaping
mouths—O city of innocents joined hand to hand
what are your thoughts as you halt in your travels
of this retarded world your zoo, aquarium and circus!

O city of the family shoe store of sliding ladders of
Buster Browns of brogues and pumps of the five and
dime of the Woolworth's luncheonette of the
Smoke 'n' Joke Shop of plastic barf and black soap and
whoopee cushions and flies in ice cubes and itching
powder of the Chinese corner grocery scene of untold
petty larcenies of the Bayeux tapestry room at Woodward's

department store of the Odeon the Paramount and the
Columbian of the Chinese mom 'n' pop dollar ninety-five
two eggs white or brown toast sausage or bacon home fries
and coffee breakfast—

O city of sockeye Salmonbellies of Thursday night
lacrosse game punch ups of cross checks and hacking
slashes of bloody noses—O city of the sprained ankle
and the broken collar bone of bent hickory sticks of leather
webbing of thunderous wood flooring of Goss and
Parnell and d'Easum of cannon shot white rubber
balls—

O city of boarding houses and lost souls of brick roads
and trolley tracks buried beneath the asphalt of
precipitous avenues of Holy Trinity Cathedral of cracked
bells in the smouldering ruins of 1898 of paddle wheelers
and steam locomotives and horse teams—O city of picks
and shovels when will your gold rush end? When will you
tear up your sidewalks and recover your stolen bank notes?
When will your Sappers be allowed to go home? When will
you free your penitents? When will your Union Jack come
down? When will your Colonel Moody hang up his regimental
tunic? O city of the dead when will you bury your dead?

O Tilt-A-Whirl city—O city of the Yo-Yo of the Pirate Boat of
the Caterpillar of the Round Up—O city of Fabergé egg
Mississippi river boat carousels of hydraulics and grease of
clitoral pink and eye shadow blue and cherry red of hydraulic
Meccano rides of transvestite construction equipment of
cotton candy and the Fun House of toothless digger
buckets of crown and anchor theft of barkers and
lever throwing carnies of the hum of generators and
hallucinogenic merry-go-round music and the kewpie

doll come-ons of three for a buck of place your bets
of the whirling Hammond B3 screams of girls screaming
at the sound of themselves screaming of popcorn wagons
and hot dog stands and greasy burgers—O city of centrifugal
forces—O empty digger bucket city—O city of spinning
lights of air brush tattoo clown art of Sno cones of candy
striped tents of taffy apples—O city of the Vomitron of
the Pukinator of the Barf-A-Go-Round—O swirling screams
—O spinning smells—O musical whirligigs—O spin cycle city
—O city of round-tipped darts and sucker odds of no-chance
shooting galleries and loaded dice—O when will the milk
bottles fall?—O when will the silver stay in the saucers?
—O when will the biggest stuffed bear be won?

O city of stationmasters and carpenters of funeral directors
and shoe sellers of car salesmen and harbour masters of teachers
and barrister-solicitors—O city of millwrights and nurses of
ministers and clerks of physician-surgeons of stevedores and
trainmen of waitresses and prison guards—O city of bootleggers
and fish canners of longshoremen and bartenders of taxi drivers
and short order cooks—

O city of cricket matches of white trousers of rolled up
shirtsleeves of wickets and innings of handlebar moustaches of
gin and quinine and tea—O straight laced city of perpendicular
avenues and streets—O colonial outpost with aristocratic aspirations!
O city of the Duke of Connaught of Lord Carnarvon of
Sir Herbert Spencer and Sir Edward Bulwer Lytton!
O the promises they made! O the plans you laid! O royal city
where is your royalty? O capital city where is your legislature?
O terminal city where is your terminus?
O garden city where is your Royal Agricultural & Industrial Fair?

O city of nervous men in red trousers of the ace of spades
and gunpowder pressed between anvils of a long pole with
a molten point—O city of archaic explosions of anvil salutes
of nervous men in red trousers of playing cards and gunpowder
and molten points—O city of bowdlerized pagan festivities of
May Queens and her courts of dancing The Lancers and may poles—
O city of ribbon festooned phalluses and skipping children—
O how have you evaded the censure of millennia of pious
hypocrites? Where is the church? Where are the feminists?
O city of missionaries and the honourably discharged and
stiff upper lippers who crushed the potlatch and toppled
the totem and showed the heathen Godless that phallus
skipping children and barrel whisky and exploding anvils
were the keys to the kingdom of heaven—

O city of spring days in back alleys of wind in the
hundred foot Emily Carr canvases of waving green boughs
up where the crows convene—O days of glimpses of yards
through hedgerows of laurel and privet and cedar of primrose
and forsythia of horse chestnut of Japanese cherry and plum
of crocuses and daffodils of azaleas and hydrangea of
columbine and pyracanthas of ruinous morning glory and
mountainous holly bushes of rotted fences of wild rose—

O soccer pitch days when the Coast Mountains looked on
and the log boomed river watched—O days of bloody knees
and ankle bunched socks—O days of half-time hands sticky
with sucked-dry oranges—O charley horse days! O bruised
shin days! O days of sudden testicular shock!
O summer days of long curved stalks of hollyhocks of
peonies of morning glory of snap dragons of violets and
campanula of lily of the valley—O city of rhododendron
the colour of old ladies' dresses of climbing rose of clematis
and japonica—O empty August days—O late afternoons of

heat releasing sidewalks—O concrete heat!—O watery cold of
Rocky's corner store's pop cooler—O dripping bottle of Coca-Cola
O parched brown grass and drooping boulevard trees
O downing the pharmaceutical cure-all in a single tilt
O city of icy brown sweet effervescence!

O city of bicycle repair shops of wealthy illiterates of
coin operated Laundromats—O city of mini-boxes of Tide
of brown stubby beer bottle return depots of
parlours of pizza of parlours of beer of parlours of
beauty—O coiffure city of the perm of the set and of
the rinse of the bowling alley—O ten-pin city of strikes
and spares of the cigarette and the beer and the
aerosol-fumigated two-toned leather sliding shoes of
the Ford and the GM dealerships—O city of gleaming
new models of the sticker price of the wind-whipped
plastic streamers of the triple—O hamburger sauce—
O city of the White Spot of car attendants ferrying
trays of burgers of fries of chocolate shakes of clam chowder—

O city of Maisie MacKenzie and Barbara MacKay—
O fierce spinster guardians of the gates of Queen's Park!
O Cerberus's of Park Lane and Pelham Street!
O steely eyed no-fool-suffering tweed-skirted Victorias!
O strict disciplinarians of the old school of wooden pointer of
white chalk of black board and rote of attendance and quiet of
sit still of pay attention and of detention—O wise teacher
sisters guardians of the gates—O sisters of south seas teak
and mahogany of linens and antimacassars of silver tea
services of lemon oiled shine—O spotless dustless rooms of
antiquity of shelves overflowing with figurines of English
bone China of Royal Crown Derby and Wedgwood of
sterling flatware in velvet lined chests of rails of souvenir
plates—O Jubilees! O Coronations! O vigilant guardian ladies

of House of Windsor teaspoon collections—O sensible shoed
tartan skirted spinster gate guardian sisters of mother's
bedroom of her good heavy sterling vanity set of Irish linen
of mother's lemon oiled mahogany dresser of sealed
afterlife chambers and macabre spiritualist séance mausoleum
preservation of awaiting her return after thirty-two years
on the other side—

O forsaken city when will you admit you miss the Indians?
O bypassed city when will you tear down apartments to
make room for forests? O spinster city when will you invade
Burnaby and conquer Coquitlam? O tough luck city when will
you kick Sir Edward Bulwer Lytton hard in the balls?

Beautiful Century

At a corner table in Paris's Lescure
over monkfish, confit de canard,
and a Côtes du Rhône,
a gentleman philosopher said:
"Life's beauty is death, for death
limits life, thus giving it meaning."
Which put in mind the battlefields
of the Somme, visited the day before.
"If so," I thought, "we saw a lot
of beauty yesterday."

Far Reaches

I reach for you
not because you are here
but because
one day you will not be.

Try as I do
to live in the present
the past
will not stay there.

Tantramar Marshes

Grass ocean.
Rusting cars.
Cow pastures.
Grey barns.
Blue herons.
Submerged fridges.
Fallen fence posts.
Rusted wire.
Grazing cows.
Railway line.
Steel silence.
Creosote stench.
Stillness.
Sackville.
Purple flowered lilacs
perfuming the air.
A church steeple
lit by lightning.
Rain.

Ganges, Saltspring Island

Dusty air of dry July
grass turned to straw
and dirt to powder.

A pickup truck
stacked high with firewood
tilts over a ditch.

A salvaged channel buoy
now marks the entrance
to a parking lot.

A water bucket for dogs
warms on the sidewalk
in front of Mouat's Dry Goods.

A war memorial in the park
promises to never forget
long forgotten men.

At a crosswalk
time winds its pocket watch
and another hundred years begins.

In Memoriam

After Satie's death they found
in his cramped apartment
two grand pianos sans strings,

dozens of soiled celluloid collars,
stacks of unopened, dusty letters
and two hundred black umbrellas.

When it rains in Paris
memorials to Erik Satie
spring up everywhere.

Mistress Muse

You and I, we have the past
It grows younger every day
We never had a future
Let us bow our heads and pray.

For the past has a future
But the future has no past
And the past goes on forever
But the future will not last.

Let us not look to the future
Let us turn our backs on it
Let us bury the future
For we have no use for it.

Let us bow our heads and pray
Let us re-imagine yesterday
Let us dwell in what was done
Let tomorrow never come.

The future has no prospects
Outside the confines of the past
The future is a dubious when
Then's then is unsurpassed.

You and I, we have a past,
Let us travel there at last
Let us go and live among
Songs that we have sung.

For the past has a direction
And knows where it has been
But the future is forever lost
And its course is unforeseen.

Let us always be together
In the once-upon-a-time
The past keeps the promises
The future must decline.

We have never had a future
But we have a tempting past
Why test an unknown yet-to-be
When was is rich and vast?

In the past, you and I
Are together every way
We never had a future
Let us bow our heads and pray.

We Shall Not Come This Way Again

Then it was a release
like throwing open a window
into a garden's green air.

Now it's closer to going,
more like a door slamming shut
than a window thrown open.

Rain Bird

Spring rain summons the plovers
or the plovers summon the rains.
Plover is lover and plum,
plump and breast round.
It is plough, plume, and hover,
gravel, grave, and unravel.

Little Birds

The little birds come
across darkening fields of snow
out of grey sky
out of purple-brown trees
over split rail fences
at day's end they come
the little birds.

See, they are almost here.

Sugar Water

Absent any searing
insight
into the nature
of existence
the idle poet
watched a hummingbird
glaring at him
in order—apparently!—
(as it later dawned
on the poet)
to draw his attention
to the fact
that the feeder
was again empty
of sugar water—
thereby
providing the poet
with an insight
(not necessarily searing
but an insight
nevertheless)
into the existence
of nature.

Breathe Deeply

If the perfume from the bouquets on the lilac bush
seems extra wonderful this spring
it is simply because all winter long I pissed on it.

Cocktail Hour

The sun retires and the dust settles
in the quarter of an hour at day's end.
In the quarter of an hour at day's end
the streets are suspended in honey.
The whisky comes out of the cupboard
in the quarter of an hour at day's end
and the revolver comes out of the drawer.

The Glass Hammer

In his windowless penthouse
he sips a non-alcoholic martini
from a wire bowl
and recalls the glass hammer
given to him by a blind regular
of the stripper bars
in "commemoration of the tears
Lindberg did not cry for his son."
He has tried all sorts of nails
but only the rubber ones work.

Cheryl

She claimed to be
overcoming old fears
leaving the past behind
finding inner peace
and all that shit.
It seemed plausible
until she opened
her carotid artery
with a utility knife.
Some of her things
went to Goodwill
and the rest
was destined
for the curb
on garbage day
including her
favourite armchair
but the thought
of a junk picker
touching it
was sickening
so I took it.
At the memorial
her books sat
in boxes on the floor.
A sign read:
Help yourself, please.

Midden

The old roller mill on the hill
is as empty as a church on Monday.
At the soft thud of a footstep
or the pinched creak of a stair
the slumbering past shifts
in its deep leather club chair.
What little sunlight enters
withers, dies and gathers dust.

There is no more wheat to hull
and no more oats to flatten.
The No. 3 Eureka Seed Cleaner
has cleaned its last seed.
The endless belt elevator is ended
and rust does not augur well.
Thompson's Grading Purifier & Seperator
purifies & separates no more.

The hoppers and the shakers
are full of nothing but dust.
The Controllable Swing Shifter
will have to shift for itself.
The weigh scale weighs gravity
and the grindstone grinds time.
Greey's Improved Vibratory Feeder
can never be improved upon.

Who's next for the midden?
Who will join the forgotten?
Wm. Gates Microscopic Software Co.?
What once miraculous inventions

await unvisited dusty rooms?
S. Jobs & Sons Memorizer & Counter?
Whose patented marvel-of-the-age
is tomorrow's comical relic?

Fitz Hugh Sound

On the lee side
of Calvert Island
aboard a 25-foot
aluminum welded
centre console
fishing boat
its Yamaha 130s cut
its trolling engine
churning a pale green slipstream
downriggers out
cannonballs 100 feet deep
lines tight
rods bowed
three dead coho
bleeding in the box
a fourth
under us somewhere
hungry for herring
and any second now
a rod tip will whipsaw
a salmon will leap
and its living energy
will go coursing
through the line
but right now
there's only raindrops
pinging
on the undulating veneer
of the ocean.

Good Hope

The cannery stands
on pilings
along the shore
of a sheltered bay.
Behind it
a marshy hillside
yet to heal
from the loss
of trees logged
a century ago.

Here stood
the bunkhouse
of Chinese men
who butchered
sockeye salmon
in the summers
at the end
of Queen Victoria's reign.

What remains of
the house
is buried in the hillside
where a creek drops
through a series
of pools and ledges
under salmonberry bushes
and around
the rotted carcasses
of cedar trees.

Here a broken bottle
diverts trickling water,
a brick keeps a mud bank
from collapsing
and a vial
once containing opium
rests on the sandy bottom
of a shallow pool,
its only blemish
a nick in the lip
of its fluted neck.

In the vial
men recline on bunks,
drawing smoke
from the bowls
of porcelain pipes,
kerosene lamps
cast dragon shadows
on the walls,
cups of black tea steam,
and dozens
of primed alarm clocks
count the seconds
to the morning's
slaughter.

Homburg Hats

Once it was amusing
to open a decaying
photo album
and look back
at the folks
glued to its pages
in their dark suits
and homburg hats,
pouter pigeon blouses
and ankle length dresses
horse drawn carriages
and clunky bikes
soup strainer moustaches
and lacy parasols
recumbent in long grass
paddling a canoe
or posing with a joke
of an automobile
But now that we are
even older
than most of those people
portrayed were then
we can feel the glue
hardening us to the pages
of our own decaying
photo album.

Amaranth

Nothing important is ever lost
Things of value resurface
The world remembers
Each artefact is catalogued
The child's doll and the golden dagger
The sunken brigantine and plundered art
The poet's trunk of unpublished poems
The world is a vast catalogue within a vault within a perfect memory
Things go not to oblivion but to safekeeping
The world protects the things it loves
Whatever was will be again
Things disappear for the sake of reappearing
The world's memory performs its magic acts
Gone is temporary
Lost is only misplaced
Whatever was will be again
Time is compound interest
The unappreciated in its own day time renders priceless
Whatever was taken for granted time grants immortality
The glacier gives back
The sand blows away
The water recedes
The world preserves matter that matters most
It shields its treasures from the sun
It holds them, their value appreciating
Until an age capable of appreciation
If it goes missing it will be found
The world remembers what it creates
It is a sleight of hand giving and retracting
Showing and hiding, putting away and taking out

The world is vaults and cupboards
Attics and tombs, sands and seas, cabinets and boxes
It preserves, it holds in trust
In middens, fire pits, archives and attics
Roman coins, skulls and Pharaohs' tombs.

Hunter

Overnight the wind
tore the patio umbrella
from its mooring,
blowing it halfway
across the lawn.
I retrieved it
and wound it down,
remembering
the spring day
when it went up.
Out of habit,
I'd left the kitchen
door open.
Only the day before
our old cat
would have
appeared at it,
ready to begin
her ritual
morning patrol.
But she would not
be going out
ever again
and instead
brown leaves
had blown in.
I examined them
in the palm
of my hand
as if I might find

the answer
to the overwhelming
question.

Just one problem

I'd quit this
life for a
fuck-it-all
adventure
if only I
didn't know
I'd waste it
agonizing over
what I'd left
behind.

Bigwin Inn

She was the pride of a rich man
so overflowing with loneliness
he had to build her to house it all.

His loneliness filled 284 rooms,
a rotunda, a dancing pavilion,
a boathouse and a golf course.

But his loneliness grew and so
he added tennis courts, bungalows,
cottages, and a watchtower.

From his watchtower he looked out
over thousands of acres
of green pine and loneliness.

On clear blue days he watched
the sky for signs of loneliness
blowing in from the west.

On cloudy days he watched
the sky for hints of rain
about to fall like loneliness.

Guests arrived by steamer
with hundreds of trunks full
of loneliness and cotton finery.

All summer long they came,
contagious with the heat of big cities,
delirious with loneliness.

They came for the piney air,
the spring water, and the boiled
halibut in loneliness sauce.

They came by the steamer load,
week after week, in the thousands,
year after year, summer after summer.

The jazz age checked in,
the Depression was a guest,
WWII stayed for a month.

He built more bungalows and
cottages, he boiled more halibut,
but his loneliness increased.

Nothing could contain it.
It was bigger than Babe Ruth,
bigger than Bobby Jones.

It was bigger than Vaudeville,
bigger than Standard Oil,
bigger than the New Deal.

So he went up into his tower
and surveyed his loneliness
and had a heart attack.

Well, nothing is bigger than death.
All his loneliness collapsed
like air sucked out of a paper bag.

Other owners came and went,
other times passed through,
but what she once had was gone.

Now she had his loneliness.
She ached with loneliness
in all her bones like arthritis.

Disco dancing marked the end
of blue loneliness and green pines.
Her boiled halibut days were over.

She'll never see another egg sauce,
never again the steamer trunks
and gentlefolk in cotton finery.

Dr k efre h ng Co a- ola!

As earth and sky
squeeze sun dry,
its light dissolving
like lemon juice
in a pitcher
of sugar water,
all summers dissolve
into one summer's eve
to be drunk down
as the painted
soft drink sign
is drunk down
by the thirsty
red brick wall
of the Armstrong
Hardware Building
Erected 1905.

The Massacre Confirmed Our Worst Suspicions

We thought we were unsinkable
until the iceberg did us in.
We thought we stood on solid ground
until the earth began to shake.

We thought it was an upswing
until it went into reverse.
We thought we had the time
but it turned out time had us.

We thought you'd heard it from him
but it was he who'd heard from you,
from such a small misunderstanding
such awful consequences grew.

We thought we finally had it right
but we were wrong all along.
We thought we had it figured out
but we didn't have it figured in.

We thought we'd take a shortcut
and they're looking for us still.
We thought we'd get another shot
but that wasn't in the drill.

We thought we had the answers
until questions started cropping up.
We thought we had a future
but the past came up so fast.

We thought that it would save us
but what it did was enslave us.
We thought it would be funny
but we vomited instead.

We thought we could escape
but couldn't figure out from what.
We thought we had it by the tail
until we took a horn in the gut.

We thought that it was over
but it had only just begun.
We thought that it was daybreak
but it was the setting of the sun.

On 7 Mile Beach

Were I a painter
I would paint you
in the early morning light
raking the long needles
of the wheat-mallows.

I would paint you
on the coral sand
by the sea
in the soft light
of the early morning.

I would paint you
in your tan shirts
and black pants
skimming the needles
into coffee-brown rows.

I would paint you
in the early morning light
raking coral dust
into the green shadows
of the wheat-mallows.

I would paint you
and your long rakes
in your blacks and tans
in the wheat-mallow morning
of the early green shade.

The Sea Rasps The Shore

The sea rasps the shore
with metronomic regularity,
filing sand, filling the ear
with its invariant obsession.

It sandpapers sleep,
scratches at the edges
of consciousness,
induces a slight nausea.

All this of course is blasphemy.
The sea "laps" at the shore,
relaxing every muscle
with its Brahms-like lullaby.

But I hear a cat
clawing at a door,
a child clutching
at his mother's dress.

I rise and navigate
darkness to the balcony.
Something out there
will not stop wanting in.

The True Line

There are many ways to go mad.
One is to sit on a Tortuga beach
staring out intently over the sea
trying to make out the true line
where blue water meets blue sky.
The eyes fight the effort furiously,
the mind revolts at the attempt,
and dizziness quickly overcomes.

The eyes refuse to see the point
in telling one blue from another.
They dislike the two shades.
They tire of creating the illusion
that you live sphere in sphere.
Have it your way: a blue screen
accepting any projected scene
or a set painter's artful scrim.

The horizon's sheer simplicity
is ludicrous and unreasonable,
unreachable and unattainable.
A clever coy disappearing act.
The eyes know trying to find
the one true line
where sky and water meet
is a coral reef to the mind.

Where The Heart Is

You, children of Loreto,
With your white teeth and laughter,
My heart is with you
In your father's truck.

You, pelicans of Cortez's Sea,
With your piercing dives,
My heart is with you
Like a fish in your gullets.

You, woman of the church,
With your shawled head,
My heart is with you
Like the beads of a rosary.

You, finches of the breakfast table,
With your pilfering flights,
My heart is with you
In the bougainvillea.

Pier Divers

Heads up, here they come,
the young bronze gods approach
on the wings of a rising tide.

Here they come, idols of
the swift green sea,
the knife bright sun.

Here they come, seven in all,
soon to mount the barnacled ladder,
soon to tread the slippery rail.

Here they come, make way,
give them their platform,
the sleek skinned, the muscular.

Here they come, stand back,
the cooing pigeons flutter,
the bikinied girls huddle.

Here they come—at last!
to tie the air in knots,
to slit the running sea.

Sweet Little Bird

Ever since you got it
Your little yellow canary
It's all I can think about
Your sweet little canary
Your sweet yellow bird.

But it won't sing for you
Your little yellow canary
Why won't it sing for you?
Your sweet little canary
Your sweet yellow bird.

Maybe it will sing for me
Your sweet little canary
Maybe I can make it warble
Your dear sweet canary
Your little yellow bird.

O come out, little bird
And spread your wings
Come out and sing
Sing a sweet song for me
O sweet, sweet, little bird!

Vanity

It was one of those days
when life was an 18th century essay
on the vanity of everything.

An aging man beseeches the good times god

Did I not the sacraments
of wine and weed perform?

Did I not honour thee
with my soul and liver?

Did thee not once lift me
into wanton wild stratospheres?

O, immortal god of revelry
why hast thee forsaken me?

Everything Becomes Housing

The grandstand
stands no more.
A Priestly Demolition crew
has razed the racetrack.
The horses are gone
and the wickets closed.
In place of the old track
is a new tract of housing.

The farmhouse
is boarded up.
The barn is empty
and the cornfield
that withstood
freezing and drought
couldn't weather subdivision.

All the streets in the city run uphill from the river

It might have been anywhere
but it was the corner of Fourth & Victoria
at 2:36 Sunday morning.
I was alone.
More importantly, I was feeling alone,
but it's not important.
I was at the bottom of a cliff
also known as an apartment building.
A block of fluorescent light filled its lobby.
It shone like a beacon of despair.
This was light with mass and corners
trapped for eternity in a box with an elevator door
and a stack of uncirculated circulars on the floor.
Einstein couldn't have explained it.
My presence at the corner of Fourth & Victoria
made the street even emptier than it was.
Before I came along it had a chance.
Now it was doomed.
I was 25 years old
and my entire death was in front of me.

I had been drinking at the Russell Hotel
and now I had nothing more to drink.
A bootlegger we had known in high school,
"Bob" of "Bob's Mobile Tune Ups",
who'd deliver any week of the day,
suddenly delivered himself
to the front porch of my mind.
Actually, it was not so much Bob,

it was more what he represented:
the door-to-door salesman,
the addiction profiteer.
Thinking of this made me as sad as a square
of Einstein-stumping fluorescent light
in an empty lobby that was never not empty.

So I thought instead of a girl.
If she had been where Fourth
crests the hill at Tipperary Park
I would have been all right.
But she was not where Fourth Street crests the hill
at Tipperary Park
and so I would not be all right.
Where was she?
Had I lost her?
Had I ever had her?
No, I had never had her.
Was she mine?
Yes, in the sense that a girl not yours is yours alone.

I turned and looked back at the river.
There it was, a black ribbon
running behind the Army & Navy store
and a derelict movie theatre.
It was a quarter mile wide
and a hundred feet deep
and yet it did not make the slightest sound.
All that water, billions of gallons,
flowing silently.
Its silence did not seem possible.
The Einstein of rivers could not explain it.
All the streets in the city run uphill from it.

I suppose all the streets in the city run downhill as well,
but I'd never experienced it.

Fourth Street had retained its paving bricks.
The bricks were as smooth as old coins,
unbeatable for traction in the rain.
Unfortunately, it was not raining.
Two parallel lines ran down its centre,
marking the position
of the old Inter-urban railway line.
The rails were gone, replaced by blacktop.
Ribbons of blacktop in a street of bricks.
That's progress for you.
It was all very interesting
in the way that uninteresting things
are sometimes interesting.
It was also very depressing
in the way that history
is very depressing.
It was every time I'd ever been alone
when I didn't want to be alone
jammed into one moment of aloneness.
Of course, I wasn't really alone.
I had myself, after all.

Contemplating the apartment building
it occurred to me that years before
I had been in its upper reaches
drinking beer with a few friends
from the glory days.
That night had been the first I'd seen of them
in years of aimless drift.
Where were they now?

Not at the corner of Fourth & Victoria.
It was just me
and a box of florescent light
on a brick paved street
where the Inter-urban railway
no longer ran
and where
farther along
at the crest of the hill
a girl I'd never had
wasn't waiting for me.

The Owl In The Midnight Tree

My back is wrenched
and my knee is buggered
and I'm way overdue
for another heart attack,
so yes, pour me a Chardonnay,
the oakier the better
and while you're up,
if you wouldn't mind,
can you spare a Tylenol 3?

Oh, the sea floods in
under berm and dyke
and our houses swim
on gravel and sand.

I'm too young to retire
and too old for this shit,
and as for my wife
I think she left me
about ten years ago,
but I'll have to check with her
because I really don't know,
so yes, pour me another Chardonnay,
the oakier the better.

Oh, the tide is turning
and the owl in the midnight tree
knows what time it is
and turns his head away.

Ala Moana Ditch

Next time
you're crossing
the bridge
over the
concrete ditch
between Ala Moana boulevard
and the park
look over
the railing
at the
speckled fish
among
the broken bottles
and syringes.

Ala Wai Boat Harbour

Don't know where
the journey began
or why
or how long ago
or what happened
along the way
but when I saw
the dead dog
on the pavement
beside the car
and the driver's door open
and the bundled
clothing and crap
piled on the roof
and the cops
trying to see
who or what
was inside
I knew where
the journey ended.

Oh, the tide is turning
and the owl in the midnight tree
knows what time it is
and turns his head away.

Sweet Ride

As good
as it feels
to ride
in a Porsche
at sunset
along the
Pali Highway
after a day
on the beach
at Lanakai,
nothing compares
to malasadas
at Leonard's
among plumeria
and neon signs
with zebra doves
at your feet
and little
Hawaiian finches
trying to score
their next
sugar fix.

Old Waikiki

On Kuhio Street you can see old Waikiki.
It has a lava rock facade
and faded but not forgotten
Art Deco aspirations.
It has a crumpled wad of bills
and some loose silver in its thrift store pants.
It needs a shave and a haircut.
It looks like it hasn't eaten since last Monday.
Old Waikiki isn't paying much attention
to the Ritz going up across Kuhio.
Old Waikiki is fishing in the Ala Wai Canal
or nursing a Schlitz in a bar
next to a tattoo parlour.
Old Waikiki has a pension cheque
coming in a day or two.
It knows this old lady
asking $350 for an '83 Malibu.
Despite everything
old Waikiki is hanging in there
pretty good.

Kodachrome Microtome

It's almost sixty years
since a shutter sectioned
one-sixtieth of a second
from 1958, capturing
a garden party, grandparents,
aunts, uncles and a
two-year-old boy,
a freshly minted
Christian soldier,
eyes level with the top
of a linen covered table,
about to pilfer
a date square.

Ultimate Futility

I helped him carry a new
dishwasher into our kitchen
and after installing it
we stood on the front porch
and he mentioned a sister
he hadn't seen in seven years
and a brother dying of cancer
and I talked about my chronic
lack of money and getting old
and we understood each other
about the ultimate futility of the
whole enterprise
and about a week later
while playing tennis
he turned to his partner
and said: "I'm going down"
and fell dead of what they call
a Hollywood heart attack.
I was thinking about this
the other night when my wife
reprimanded me for still doing
the dishes by hand.

Moving Out

I never wanted to sell it, she says
about her hillside house in Cadboro Bay.
I love this house. This is my house.
Should I have kept it? I don't know.
But it's too late now. It's gone.
I wanted a view of the bay, but it's
blocked by trees and mansions.
You can't be serious, I think,
tangled up in an armchair
stubbornly resisting
the open space between doorjambs.
Why should they have the view to themselves?—
I say chop down the trees and burn the houses!
A vision of her at the helm of a Viking ship.
I need a chainsaw, I say, half joking,
trying yet another angle of attack.
Before I leave I'm going to pick all the fruit!
Yes, I laugh, plunder the yellow plum.
That'll teach the new owners!
They bought my house, but not my plums!
I'm going to take them all and make jam!
Jars and jars of jam! Yellow plum jam!
At last, the chair tumbles
clear of the doorjambs,
landing on the hardwood
with an empty hallway thud.

Road Safety

Driving yesterday
past the site
of his elementary school
he thought he saw
a soccer ball
come bouncing suddenly
across the road in front
causing a hard brake
and a bump
from the car behind
but the expected boy
did not appear
racing blindly
after the ball
and he saw
that neither would there be
a trip to the principal's office
a lecture on road safety
or a leather strap sharply
across the boy's
upturned palm.

Racing Time

All those years
running like crazy
to stay out in front
or at least alongside
but it passed us
the other day
at a pace
we could not match
and now we watch
as it accelerates
ever farther ahead
becoming smaller
and smaller
as we fall farther
and farther back.

New Roof

We laid tar paper and shingles
according to my brother's exacting standards,
applied liquid rubber under the overlaps,
and hammered in extra nails on the windward side
as if we were restoring the dome of a Medieval cathedral
and not a shoe boxy, shiplapped,
single car garage from the Great Depression
repurposed in the '50s
as our family's summer cottage's extra bedroom,
card den, swim suit changing room,
and comic book depository.
But shortly after our precision roofing work
the property was sold
and the new owner's excavator
smashed to pieces any remaining illusions.

Martyrdom

Everyone has an axe to grind,
everyone has a complaint,
everyone's been victimized
and everyone's a saint.

Everyone was a target,
everyone is a casualty,
everyone's been fucked around
and everyone's an injured party.

Everyone deserves an apology,
everyone merits restitution,
everyone wants the Supreme Court
to amend the constitution.

Everyone's beef is legitimate,
everyone's grievance is real,
no one else will ever know
how terrible we feel.

Everyone's a wounded bird,
everyone was abused—funny,
how everyone will take the cash
but it's not about the money.

Everyone's blood is boiling,
everyone against everyone,
and everyone must pay for
the wrong we've all been done.

Everyone wants justice
so let everyone proclaim,
that every cause is righteous
and everyone's to blame.

Queensborough Landing

Where a man stands
on a platform
over the river
watching two loons
cut across the wake
of tugs towing a log boom,
a lumber mill once stood
with jack ladders, green chains,
saw blades, kilns,
mountains of hog fuel
and acres of lumber
stacked thirty feet high.

My Ship

The day I was born
was the day
my ship came in.
She was all the luck
a boy could want
but she sailed
the next day
for other ports
and I don't believe
she's ever coming back.

Little Fish

While big business
is conducted
in the boardroom,
leaves submerged
in the courtyard pool
circle back slowly
to the jet, which
shoots them forward
like little fish
darting in a stream.

Intersection

The corner
of 3rd avenue
and 2nd street
was deserted
that Saturday
in August of '69,
the last weekend
before grade 7.
Except for
faint hissing
in my ears,
it was quiet,
making me wonder
where everyone
had gone.
No rain in weeks
and the grass
in the boulevard
was brown
and the elms
were dry
and their leaves
were dusty
and there were
no birds
at the corner
of 3rd avenue
and 2nd street
on a Saturday
in August of '69,

the last weekend
before grade 7.

Brothers of the long table

We gather now as then
seemingly haphazardly
but in reality in a kind of
subconscious choreography
arriving forty years later
in the same order
at the same times
to take our same places
at the long table.
One leaves in a few weeks
to climb a mountain in Nepal,
another lost his voice
to a rare neurological disorder,
three are still practicing law,
and eight are retired,
but we are all still bewildered
still in thrall
to the same delusions
although their grip on us
is starting to loosen.
In the midst of the
beer and bullshit
we wonder if we should
have come tonight
and pledge to skip it
next year—the same old crap
by the same old boys
on the same old night
in the same old town—
who needs it, really?
Why go out once a year

on a foggy night in December?
Don't we have somewhere else
we'd rather be—like in bed
with that book we started to read
a couple or three years ago
by what's his name
the guy who wrote
that other thing we liked?
Or? Or? Or where else?
But the answer to the question
is the same tonight
as forty years ago—
what better place to be
bewildered and delusional
than among the aging brethren
of the long table.

Cliff Dwellers of Los Angeles

A billion square feet of retail space ends
where men wearing garbage bags
wheel shopping carts along the cliff
as if the ocean were a supermarket
brimming with happiness and success
and not a restless blue insanity.

Investigation of a Woman's Brassiere and a Bent Cane Chair

A woman has tossed her brassiere
over the back of a bent cane chair.

The weight of a brassiere tossed
over the back of a bent cane chair
can easily overturn an empire.

But a woman will throw off her brassiere
as if it were merely a brassiere.

A bent cane chair is used as a prop in a play
about a woman unhooking her brassiere.

The moral of the play:
a woman and her brassiere are soon parted.

A bent cane chair has no arms
whereas a woman has two,
thus law and order prevail.

A brassiere, infused with the fragrance
of a woman's skin, reposes over a bent cane chair.

Obviously a woman has placed her brassiere
as a decoy over the back of a bent cane chair.

Suppose a woman meant to toss her brassiere
over the back of bent cane chair, but it slipped,
causing an army to march to its death.

The noun brassiere should be italicized
except when flung carelessly
over the back of a bent cane chair.

There are two kinds of brassiere in the world:
one of them is associated with bent cane chairs.

Antique Market

He wanted $6 a piece
for salvaged porcelain doorknobs.
An old rolling pin
was mine for $10.
19th century newel posts,
unstripped, $60 each.
Antique screen door? $95.
I asked what he wanted
for the old photograph
of a baby who,
according to words
pencilled on the verso,
"died of black diphtheria."
$2, he said.

As It Is At The Moment

You wanted me in the moment
but the moment was too fast.

You wanted me here and now
but the future condemned the past.

I tried my best to slow it down
as you tried to slow down sex.

I tried to caress the moment
stroked its hair kissed its neck

Ran my tongue along its spine
until at last my tongue ran dry.

Tried for years for centuries
but no slowness could satisfy.

Something pushed me forward
something I could not deflect

something always commanded
kill this moment for the next.

i like your parents' liquor store, baby

i like santa monica
the way everything shines like new minted coins
like the hubs of a 735i
like a gold rolex
i like the promise of the morning
the restaurant where we sit
kona coffee and eggs benedict
the actors playing waiters
the bums on the sidewalk
the cut of their sleeping bags
the way they always look like rain

i like men pushing grocery carts along the cliff
the feeling i get hanging a left
the highway entrance ramp
the cliff's steady erosion
the futile attempts to shore it up
i like the drive through malibu
the burned out houses high on the hillsides and
the blackened stumps of trees
i like the liquor stores
and the ocean
and the fires that won't go out

i like your parents' place in montecito
its sepulchral chic
its serrated swiss no-stick omelette pans
its little invisible birds that twirtle
its tortuous-limbed trees
its empty tennis courts
i like the leaky showers in the changing rooms at poolside

the smell of vidal sassoon
the hot tub and the glossy magazines
and i like your hair
i like its coarseness
it makes me think of sugarcane and wheat
it is a fine crop of hair and i like it

i like the way you sprint on a beach
i like your stride
i like it because it is not a woman's stride
i like your legs
i like them because they are a woman's legs
i like your hair
its sepulchral chic
the blackened stump of your tennis club
your sugarcane and your endless fields of grain
your thirst
your glossy legs
i like your malibu and your entrance ramp
your shopping carts and your riding crop
and i like your parents' liquor store, baby

i like the bar of the montecito hotel
its big gaudy flowers and its burning logs
old tuxedos hitting on old broads
the nut brown ale i'm served
the salted peanuts
looking at you looking at me
the tension mounting
when the joke isn't funny anymore
the acting we do
the parts we play
the way we turn tuxedos and old broads into movie extras

i like your malibu
i really do
i like your salted peanuts
your burning tuxedos and your sugarcane hair
i like your stride
your fog
the dew on the leaves of the trees
that came all the way from xanadu or zululand or zanzi-
bar
i like your ocean motionless

i like sleeping alone in a small unfamiliar bed
where small unfamiliar men before me have slept
imagining the sun behind your curtains
which certain men unfamiliar to me have parted
i like your parents' place in montecito
its birds twirping in tortuous-limbed trees

its empty tennis courts
its ocean breezes
its salty peanuts
its coffee and omelettes and amulets
the secret plans for the day in your head
the map of your mind
the nape of your neck
your zululand and your burning sands
your nut brown tan and your sugarcane hair
and your stride
what can i say?
i like your parents' liquor store, baby

i like the sinuous plants that carpet the dunes
the way they cling to life
the indian graveyard

its planks and posts
the towels you spread on the sand
standing in the ocean
letting the breakers try to knock me down
i like it when the earth quakes
i like it when you say did you feel it, baby?
i like thinking of two people copulating at its epicenter
broken glass strewn all around their bed
and she says to him did you feel it, baby?
i like a natural disaster
a good shake
a stiff tsunami on the rocks
i like your one piece
i'd like to shred it into sixty

i like santa barbara
being in its mountains
their steep sides
their deep green valleys
the impression of velvet
orange and purple skies
mist pouring in off the ocean
mountains in silhouette
the death of the sun
the birth of the night
approaching headlights and suicide corners
i like it when you say you met the billionaire
who invented the cats eyes on the highways

i like him
i like you meeting him
he's a saint
he's a natural disaster
he's a double tsunami on the rocks

he's a killer on the loose
he's a rich caboose
he's the cats eyes

i like you (you know i do)
your mist
your velvet silhouette
your map for what it can't tell us
i like going nowhere with you
i like it when we always get there

i like your tortuous limbs
your trattorias hidden in trees
your gorgonzola and your cream
i like your friends
your amarone
and i like it when i ask the waiter to bring me grappa and
he brings me your shredded one piece on an unfamiliar
bed
i like your stride
your tortuous friends hidden in gorgonzola and
your grappa and your granma and
your parents' liquor store in Malibu
i like a good laugh like i like a good tsunami and
of course
i like a good italian salami

i like valet parking
a late dinner
restaurante i cugini
i like iwo jima and
the marine corps and
waiters in formal waiter attire
osso bucco and le cigar volante

i like a rare cigar
a fast car
you in candlelight shining like cats eyes
i like your warm chevre on an unfamiliar bed

i like your hospitality
your filthy herbal tea
your apartment
your deportment
jaz with one zee
your tortuous limbs
your gongonzola
your cream
your stride

i like the sound of your cliff eroding and
the sound of your palm trees laughing and
the sound of your tenor sax and
i like your malibu and your entrance ramp
your shopping carts and your riding crop
and i like your parents' liquor store, baby.

casket royale

i like a fall fair
a roadblocked main street
corn husks tied to parking meters
a good old community event
i like seeing folk
doing all the things folk do on a saturday
only all of them doing it together all at once
i like the gaunt farmers
and their mother goose fat wives
i like the single moms
and their double kids
i like the village idiots
and the local layabouts
i like the would-be businessmen
in their would-be suits
with the cuffs too long
and the arms too short
and i like the hair of the old ladies
spun on their heads
like frosted cotton candy

but most of all
i like the retarded young man
i like his grey jacket
the way it's zippered up all the way to his chin
as if there were a cold nor' wester
blowing in from some frozen bay
i like this young man
i like his friendliness
i like his grey jacket
zippered up to his chin

i like his eyes
the way the two of them can't agree on anything
i like the way he works the street
the way he thrusts out his hand to pensioners
like a politician seeking re-election
the way he doesn't know what to say
once he gets past hello hows it going today
i like the pensioner's embarrassed smiles
and hesitant handshakes
as if they were kids again
and this was a parade
and the retarded young man was their uncle
dressed as a funny clown passing out candy

i like to imagine that they knew
the retarded young man as he was growing up
knew his parents well
sometimes bought him ice creams
after church on sunday
felt in some strange way responsible
but would rather forget
now that they're getting on and all

i like that retarded young man
i admire his bravado
and the way he's got that grey jacket zippered up
it makes me think of getting one for myself
and running for office

i like the open doors
of all the shops on main street
i like the way the merchants turn out
the insides of their stores
i like the handiwork of craftspeople

i like the honey bottlers
and the jam packers
and the muffin makers
i like the 3 for a $1 paperbacks
and the hardcovers
on the state of the inland Finnish fishery 1967
i like the lemonade stand
and the barbeques grilling bavarian sausages
to the strains of the wabash cannonball
from the toe tappin' fiddlers band
making music like they always do
like it was a chore
like they'd rather be breaking rocks
in a chain gang

i like casket royale
its showroom doors flung wide
as if to say please come inside
i like the pool hall lighting
and the lemon oil atmosphere
i like the shiny new models on display
and i like thinking of the proprietor
puzzled as ever as to why
no one's kicking brass handles
or slamming lids
or getting in for a test drive
he's a helluva guy the proprietor
and i like his community spirit
and his better business bureau ethics
and his kiwanis charity
and his beautiful naive poetic heart
that admits no difference between

what he's selling
and what they're flogging at the corner coffee shop
and across the street at hazel's coiffure

i like it
i like it all
so fling wide the doors of eternity
open up and let the reaper in
it's a fine fall fair day
and there's retarded cannon balls
and fiddlers tied to parking meters
and fresh squeezed sausage
and bavarian conversation
and it's a toe tappin' autumn wabash
and everybody's welcome.

last hurrah before lights out

you have no beginning
and you have no end
you flow like viscous slate
you slide to your fate
like molten pewter
you slide to the edge

and fall
niagara

you fall like you are standing still
like spokes in a fast turning wheel
like a roulette wheel
like a crooked deal
like a movie reel
you fall quiet as an empty street
like a whisper
like a silk stocking slipping off a bed

i like the way you fall
the clever illusion you give of falling
your way of standing still
like spokes in a fast turning wheel
this silky slide over the side
i like the way you turn white as you fall
how this gives the appearance of ice
how you disintegrate
like an illusion
i like your monotony
your ever changing sameness
i like the spray you throw

your technicolor rainbows
the way your mist floats like reluctant rain

i like your gift shops
i like the way your souvenirs cascade
the way they spill over the shelves and onto the floor and out the door
i like the eternal flow of your souvenirs
the clever illusion they give of standing still
like spokes in a fast turning wheel
the way they fall quiet as an empty street
i like your capri
i like its 1950s steak house charm
its vegas vogue
its underworld cachet
i like its olympic torch facade
i like the small windows set in chrome
the way the darkness within shines through on the sunniest days
i like the menu
with its eggplant parmigiana
and its spaghetti puttanesco
with its crusty bread from rigonelli's
and its fat marbled rib eyes
i like the way the waiters say sir
i like their slicked black hair
their undertaker solemn airs

i like my rib eyes thick and rare and red
and i like a dab of brylcreem in my hair
and i like a clean ashtray
and a crisp linen napkin
and i like a woman's lipstick
thick and rare and red

and i like her teased up hair
and her shoulders bare
and her cigarettes promptly lit
well lit and promptly lit
without a word
and her ashes falling
quiet as an empty street
and the smoke rising
like fast turning wheels

i like you at twilight
your falling sun is a maudlin act
it is a sentimental favourite
but an artistic flop
and i like it very much
its reds, oranges and violets
like neon suspended in honey
it takes me back
to certain minutes of certain days
to which i would most certainly return
were return within my power
i like your falling sun
the way it falls
the way the soul rises in response
the way it activates memory
the melancholy it provokes
bittersweet like cognac
endless like rhapsody in blue
i like your twilight
the last hurrah before lights out

i like your horizontal streets
and your venetian avenues
i like your strip mall couture

and your service station flamboyance
i like your gleaming chromes
and your garden gnomes
i like the hum of your power lines
and your virgin mary shrines
i like your intersections
and your traffic lights
your 8 cylinder acceleration
and your super 8 speed
your horizontal strips
your autoerotic intersections
and your flamboyant avenues

i like your capri
i like your cocktails
your strapless gowns
and your long white cigarettes
your nicotine
and your listerine
your rib eye steaks
and your kidney stones
your hot dates
and your cyclomates
and your high flying cancer rates
i like your brylcreem charm
and your las vegas smarm
i like your flashy gold rings
and your black silk stockings
i like your milky thighs
and your red rare rib eyes
i like your eggplant parmigiana
and your twisted dry martinis
i like your boss and his bossa nova
i like your polyester and your lycra

your spandex and your fortrell
and your foto-ramic gee-whiz peep show girlie magazines

i like your sleek black limousines
how they cruise at super 8 speed
your long sleek black limousines
hearse black in the midday sun
gleaming chrome in the hot sun
your long sleek black limousines
slick and black as brylcreemed hair
the way they fall through frame
like a silk stocking slipping off a bed
like a funeral cortege
like figures in a wax museum
like petrified wood
like eggplant parmigiana on a plate
the way they stand still
your beautiful long sleek black limousines
like spokes in a fast turning wheel.

matadors of the asphalt bullring

your artificial sunlight
i like it, it's good
it complements your neon ocean
your synthetic sand
your dirty canals
your empty apartments
your wool-suited jews
sweating it out
in the sweltering pastels
in the shadows of

your swank hotels
i like their verticality
their corroded hospitality
their cocktail charm
their vacant glitz
their lounge act sincerity
their potted palms
and sweating palms
and i like the way the cleaning staffs
are choreographed
to mop your lobbies
i like the swish of a wet mop
i like a nice clean shine
i'm a sucker for a slippery when wet sign
i like your ladies in blue
i like the way they move
i like the groove
i like a firm wrist action
in syncopation with the hips

i like the stroke
and i like a dirty joke
when it comes clean
and i like a brilliant sheen

i like your russian cabbies
and your latino beauties
your toothpaste blondes
your old new yorkers come to live
and your young gays come to die
your hooker bitches
and your brackish ditches
your sour krauts
and your afro-blacks
i like it
i like a lot
because everybody's from somewhere
but nobody's from here

i like your main drag at night
the way everyone shows up
for a party no one was invited to
the way your restaurants
serve dinner on the sidewalk
i like your forty ounce margaritas
your seafood pastas
your tempura shrimp
your surf and turf
your tenderloins
your sushi-maki
your shark fin soup
your guadeloupe

i like your havana cabanas
your wrap around bars
your neon stars
your sidewalk lounges
your free floor shows
i like your male impersonators
impersonating females
impersonating celebrities
who are impersonations of singers

i like your alleyways
the slam of dumpster lids
i like your side streets
with their trees full of birds
singing like rusty hinges
i like your hooded moon
and your green coconuts
your cigar emporiums
your fashion boutiques
your low fat yogurt franchise operations
your pet lizard ladies
your jesus saves sandwich board men
your macaws on the shoulders of guys
pedalling ten speeds to salvation
i like it
i like it all
it's the cat's meow
it's turkey in the straw
it's quick draw mcgraw
it's the last hurrah

[but about your wind
i don't like it after dark
i don't like the way it eats
at the cracks in the glazing
in the windows of your hotel rooms
i don't like it
it's eerie sounding
it's spooky like a b movie
it's giving me the willies
i can't sleep
i'm going to call housekeeping
i'm going to complain
i'm going to ask them
to turn it off]

your race track
i like it, it's big
it's banked
and it goes around and around and around
i like your candy coloured cars
your logo-ed up one piece driving sheaths
your beer and tequila lubricated hot wheels
your titanium balled drivers
your rocket ship snap-on ratchet riders
your matadors of the asphalt bullring

i like the acceleration
your foot to the floor
pedal to the metal
your all out full throttle
your speed demons
your demon speeders
i like the sound of your cars
they're insanely loud

they're like old news reels
of flying fortresses spiralling down
over the father land

i like your balls and your high test testosterone
your adrenaline and your gasoline
your speed of consumption
how fast you eat up track
how quick you burn through tires
the distance between one kool and the next
the time it takes to guzzle a bud
you're about more of the same
and how much it costs
you're about the jets that get you there
and the get that jets you there
you're about money
and the speed at which it travels
the sonic boom of cash
travelling at a thousand bucks a second
the fastest thing going
faster than light
faster than light beer
faster than a gallop to marlboro country

i like your F-18s banking
your pubic address blaring
your breeze blowing through palms
and your burgers frying
i like your top guns
your top downs
your tank tops
your topless
your pot bellies
your pork bellies

your pork barrelling
your air force base
your on base
your off base
your strike 1, 2, 3
your stroke
your one under par
your get out of the car
your nasty little titty bars
your soft shoulder fellatio
your air brake blow jobs

i like your ritualized rubberized murder
of left turns all the way
on a fast track
on a hot day
i like you, florida
i really do

[but about your wind
i don't like it after dark
i don't like the way it eats
at the cracks in the glazing
in the windows of your hotel rooms
i don't like it
it's eerie sounding
it's spooky like a b movie
it's giving me the willies
i can't sleep
i'm going to call housekeeping
i'm going to complain
i'm going to ask them
to turn it off]

the gentle sleep your burnished scullery sunrise brings

your billion year old rocks
bald, broken and cracked
treed, ferned, and mossed
root-clenched, rain-drenched
the way they rise
from your lakes algonquin
like a swimmer's shoulders like a loon's head like a full moon

your lakes
their transparent indifference
their fathomless shallowness
the way they pull down unwary clouds
the way they drown unwise blue skies
the weight of your lakes beneath me
your full moon rocks
your billion year old shoulders
your cracked clouds
your root-clenched transparency
your fathomless indifference

your red and white pines
birch and speckled alder
your broken log slides and rusted bunk springs
your beaver dams and your fresh water clams
your water lilies
the loom of your loons
their weave
their tapestry of earth and air
their white on black backs

black on white bellies
your fusion of confusion
your confucian indifference

your confucian flying fish
your airmarine tapestry weavers
your subborne earth-air joiners
i like them like i like your rusted lilies
your speckled dams
your broken birches
your fresh water bunk springs
your red and white log slides
your forests
your forty eight shades of green
your toadstools
your orange mushrooms
your red berries
your marshes
the tea you steep there

and you
companion canoeist
your tales about your father
about his Gestapo and his Russian tanks
about his misplaced tools and sudden violent commands
about his letters to the editor and lectures to Jehovah's Witnesses
about his windsurfing
about booze and despair and your brother's header off the crossbar
about ritual sacrifice and Monty Python
about a Mayan king passing needles through his foreskin
about first loves and lost loves and sex slaves
i like your script

the detours of your mind
your Mayan headers off the crossbar
your booze tools and your Russian sex slaves
your lost tanks and your despairing editors
your Gestapo Witnesses passing needles through their foreskins
your windsurfing lost loves
your father's bad cooking
and the ritual sacrifice of your script
therefore bowsman
inform your king and your high priest
to bring on goats and virgins
ready the needles
loosen the foreskin
i want to sacrifice myself upon the holy toadstool
upon your father's bad cooking
upon indifferent Russian sex tools

i want to dive in algonquin
i want your billion year old rocks
your algae and leeches and your fresh water clams
i want your reeds and your murky brown bottom alive with dead trees
i want to dive in
i want your liquid embrace
your indifferent enclosure

your portages
your canoe overhead
its ever increasing weight
your bloody feet
your black creeks
treacherous stones
retreating bears

your black feet
your ever increasing stones
your bloody canoe
your treacherous overhead black bloody weight

your infuriating random symmetry
your patternless non-existent patterns
your inescapable maddening logic
the precision of your imprecision
your fallen trees fallen just so
your deer shit designer right
your faultless timing
your perfect floral arrangements

i surrender

your prevailing winds
your retarded pines
your cracked boulders
your drowned logs
your mauve sky
your purple dye
your retarded sundown
your forest drained of colour
the way you leach into a lake
your river nipissing
your moose pissing
your treacherous overhead black bloody weight

i surrender

your cracked ribs
your broken sunsets
your billion year old pines

your prevailing purples
your night
your fight or flight
the slow drip of adrenaline leaching into me like night
leaching into lake
i like a slow dissolve
a stern resolve
i bow to you

i surrender

your fight or flight
your adrenal drip
the way your emptiness empties itself into me
the fullness of your emptiness
your sundown
your night in which nothing sleeps
and everything listens
your nocturnal listeners
whom i can hear listening
within the silence of them listening

i surrender

your sunrise
its smooth old burnished block and tackle
its winch
the hoist of it
like a flag up a pole
like a matinee curtain going up
your orchestra pit
with its chipmunks playing like hungover alarm clocks
winding down
your pneumatic woodpeckers and your bassooning loons

that i like
like i like the slam of a privy door like i like a cookhouse bell
your kitchen clatter
your pots and pans and wooden spoons
your scandinavian scullery girls
your burnished peckers
your hoisted poles
your cookhouse loons and your pneumatic privies

your alarming curtains
your unconscious matinee
what i'm trying to say
i like the gentle sleep your burnished scullery sunrise brings.

Acknowledgements

I want to acknowledge first and foremost the love, support and companionship of Janet Ellis, who, despite everything, always sees things through with typically enormous generosity, patience and understanding; the creative inspiration and friendship provided continuously since 1975 by the one-and-only Darion Jones; and finally I want to acknowledge the debt I will forever owe to the beautiful, talented and irreplaceable Cheryl Lynn Swarts.

About the Author

W. Bruce MacDonald's poems have appeared in Malahat Review, Quarry, Antigonish Review, THIS Magazine, and CV2. In 1997 he won THIS Magazine's Great Canadian Literary Hunt for his poem 'i like your parents' liquor store, baby.' He has published 4 poetry chapbooks and 2 books of short stories, and is the author of *The Good Hope Cannery* and *Salmonbellies vs. The World.* Bruce has a BA from UVIC and an MA from UBC. He lives in Surrey, BC.

Printed in October 2018
by Gauvin Press,
Gatineau, Québec